W9-BAY-276

When It Comes to Bugs

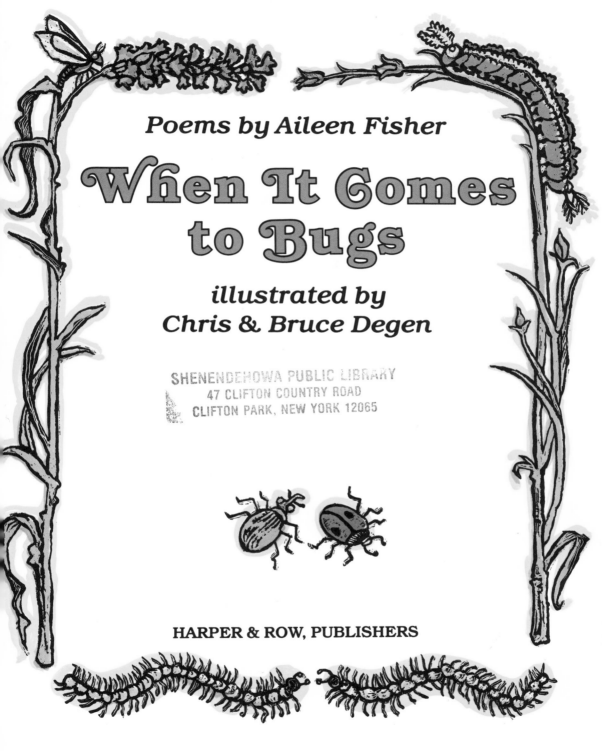

Poems by Aileen Fisher

When It Comes to Bugs

illustrated by
Chris & Bruce Degen

SHENENDEHOWA PUBLIC LIBRARY
47 CLIFTON COUNTRY ROAD
CLIFTON PARK, NEW YORK 12065

HARPER & ROW, PUBLISHERS

53998

ACKNOWLEDGMENTS
Acknowledgment is made for permission to reprint the following
copyrighted material:
"Bookish," "Mrs. Brownish Beetle," "Upside Down," from *Up the
Windy Hill*, published by Abelard-Schuman in 1953. Copyright
© 1953 by Aileen Fisher, copyright renewed 1981.
"Caterpillars," "Like a Bug," "Spider," from *Cricket in a
Thicket*, published by Charles Scribner's Sons in 1963. Copyright
© 1963 by Aileen Fisher.
"Going Barefoot" from *Runny Days, Sunny Days*, published by
Abelard-Schuman in 1958. Copyright © 1958 by Aileen Fisher.
"Little Talk" from *That's Why*, published by Thomas Nelson & Sons
in 1946. Copyright © 1946 by Aileen Fisher, copyright renewed
1974.
"Sky Net" from *In the Woods, In the Meadow, In the Sky*, published
by Charles Scribner's Sons in 1965. Copyright © 1965 by
Aileen Fisher.
"When It Comes to Bugs" from *I Wonder How, I Wonder Why*, published
by Abelard-Schuman in 1962. Copyright © 1962 by Aileen Fisher.

When It Comes to Bugs
Text copyright © 1986 by Aileen Fisher
Illustrations copyright © 1986 by Chris and Bruce Degen
Printed in the U.S.A. All rights reserved.
10 9 8 7 6 5 4 3 2 1
First Edition

Library of Congress Cataloging in Publication Data
Fisher, Aileen Lucia, 1906–
    When it comes to bugs.

    Summary: A collection of poems about different kinds
of bugs including spiders, dragonflies, ladybugs, and
many others.
    1. Insects—Juvenile poetry.   2. Children's poetry,
American.   I. Degen, Chris, ill.   II. Degen, Bruce, ill.
III. Title
PS3511.17294W5 1986   811'.52   85-45248
ISBN 0-06-021819-3
ISBN 0-06-021822-3 (lib. bdg.)

Other Books by Aileen Fisher

ANYBODY HOME?
EASTER
GOING BAREFOOT
I STOOD UPON A MOUNTAIN
LIKE NOTHING AT ALL
LISTEN, RABBIT
ONCE WE WENT ON A PICNIC
OUT IN THE DARK AND DAYLIGHT
RABBITS, RABBITS
SING, LITTLE MOUSE

Bookish

This little Bug
has a very wise look,
crawling over
the words on my book.

Of course, he can't read,
but possibly
he's looking at things
that I can't see.

Dragonflies

How do dragonflies
darting by
like flashing streaks
in the sun-bright sky
catch mosquitoes
or snatch a fly?

I'll tell you: one
of their smartest tricks
while speeding over
their bailiwicks
is making a net
of their legs—all six,

And scooping up every
last bug they spy
to eat for dinner
as they flash by
like silver streaks
in the sun-bright sky.

Woolly Bear Caterpillar

Caterpillar, have a care . . .
find a place to creep in.
Soon a chill will fill the air,
frosty nights will deepen.
How forehanded that you wear
a furry coat to sleep in!

Crickets

Of all the insects
crickets chirp
longer than any.

And I know why they *do*
at night,
bet you a penny.

Because they try
to count the stars
and, well, there are so *many*.

Mrs. Brownish Beetle

When it was October
and a hard frost came
Mrs. Brownish Beetle
(I don't know her other name)
said: "Dear me, it's chilly,"
said: "My coat is thin,"
said: "Land sakes, I'd better find
    a place to cuddle in."

So Mrs. Brownish Beetle
after several tries
found a hole beneath a stone
that was a beetle's size,
and said: "Oh my, how lucky,"
said: "How very nice,"
said: "I'll snuggle down away
    from wind and snow and ice.

"I'll set my clock at April,"
Mrs. Beetle said,
"I'll wind it up and put it here
beside my little bed."
So Mrs. Brownish Beetle
(I don't know her other name)
nestled down and went to sleep
    and slept till April came.

Spider

I saw a little Spider
with the smartest spider head:
she made—somewhere inside her—
a magic silken thread.

I saw her sliding down it.
She dangled in the air.
I saw her climbing up it
and pulling up each stair.

She made it look so easy
I wished all day I knew
how *I* could spin a magic thread
so I could dangle too.

Right-of-Way

When a Beetle
on a nettle,
crawling down
one summer day,

Meets a Beetle
on the nettle
crawling *up*
to eat a petal,

Don't you wonder
how they settle
which one has
the right-of-way?

Upside Down

It's funny how beetles
and creatures like that
can walk upside down
as well as walk flat.

They crawl on a ceiling
and climb on a wall
without any practice
or trouble at all,

While *I* have been trying
for a year (maybe more)
and still I can't stand
with my head on the floor.

About Caterpillars

What about caterpillars?
Where do they crawl
when the stars say, "Frost,"
and the trees say, "Fall?"

Some go to sleep
in a white silk case
when the winds say, "Blow!"
and the clouds say, "Race!"

Some sleep in bags
of woven brown
or curl in a ball
when the year says, "Frown."

None has the least
little urge to know
what the world is like
when the sky says, "Snow."

Sky Net

I know a busy fisherman
who fishes where it's dry.

He spreads his net
where nothing's wet.
He spreads it in the *sky*.

He doesn't care to catch a fish
that likes to swim
and splash and swish,
he only has a *spider* wish . . .
to catch a bug or fly.

Drippy Day

I wouldn't blame a Beetle-Bug
who started to complain
when the day was cloudy
and the sky began to rain:

He doesn't have a cozy house,
the lonely little fellow.
He only has a drippy leaf
to make him an umbrellow.

Going Barefoot

Ladybug,
    can you see my toes
    like five white hills
    before your nose?

Ladybug,
    does it make you giggle
    when five white hills
    begin to wiggle?

Ladybug,
    have you heard the news?
    It's June! I'm wearing
    my barefoot-shoes.

Centipede

A Centipede's a clever one,
a Centipede's no dunce . . .
getting all those feet to run
together, all at *once*.

When Mowers Pass

Beetle-folk beneath the grass
must get scared when mowers pass,
and go darting helter-skelter
looking for an air-raid shelter.

Like a Bug

Do you ever wonder
what it's like to be a bug,

Fitted in a jacket
that is stiff and rather snug,

Sleeping in a thistle
or beneath a leafy rug,

Never having gingersnaps
or cocoa in a mug,

Or a father you can talk to,
or a puppy you can hug?

When It Comes to Bugs

I like crawlers,
I like creepers,
hoppers, jumpers,
fliers, leapers,
walkers, stalkers,
chirpers, peepers . . .

I wonder why
my mother thinks
that finders can't be keepers?

Little Talk

Don't you think it's probable
that beetles, bugs, and bees
talk about a lot of things . . .
you know, such things as these:

The kind of weather where they live
in jungles tall with grass,
and earthquakes in their villages
whenever people pass.

Of course, we'll never know if bugs
talk very much at all...
because our ears are far too big
for talk that is so small.

Point of View

For little beetles
looking up
the sun is called
a buttercup.

E 811 F   53998
Fisher, Aileen Lucia,
When it comes to bugs /

$11.95 09/08/86 AEU-9428

DATE DUE

SHENENDEHOWA PUBLIC LIBRARY
47 CLIFTON COUNTRY ROAD
CLIFTON PARK, NEW YORK 12065

SHENENDEHOWA PUBLIC LIBRARY
0 00 06 0027709 9